Colorful Swearing Dreams
Swear Word Coloring Book for Adults

THIS BOOK WILL KICK YOUR STRESS AWAY BY MOTIVATING THE SHIT OUT OF YOU AND BRINGING YOUR POSITIVE THOUGHTS & SELF-LOVE UP!

Multiple studies revealed that coloring mandalas, geometric patterns & other shapes helps reduce stress and anxiety for adults.

This self-love & positive motivational swear word coloring book will allow you to enter in a relaxed state by focusing on what you are doing and blocking out the nonstop thinking or other distractions.
Those swear word designs will make you laugh, motivate you and relieve your stress by expelling your negative thoughts.

This book contains 30 pages of beautiful & intricate designs mixing up with funny **motivational swear words** that will connect with you.
Each page is single-sided for getting the best coloring experience.

TIME TO COLOR THE STRESS AWAY!

All Rights Reserved. Colorful Swearing Dreams

No part of this book may be reproduced, stored in a retrieval system, or transmitted in any form or by any means, electronic, mechanical, photocopying, recording, or otherwise, without the prior written permission of the author.

Colorful Swearing Dreams

Swear Word Coloring Book for Adults

Coloring Test Page

SHIT	FUCK	SHIT
Shit	FUCK	SHIT
SHIT	FUCK	SHIT
SHIT	FUCK	SHIT
SHIT	FUCK	SHIT
SHIT	FUCK	SHIT
SHIT	Fuck	SHIT
SHIT	FUCK	SHIT
SHIT	FUCK	SHIT
SHIT	FUCK	SHIT

Colorful Swearing Dreams

Swear Word Coloring Book for Adults

Colorful Swearing Dreams
Swear Word Coloring Book for Adults

Colorful Swearing Dreams

Swear Word Coloring Book for Adults

Colorful Swearing Dreams

Swear Word Coloring Book for Adults

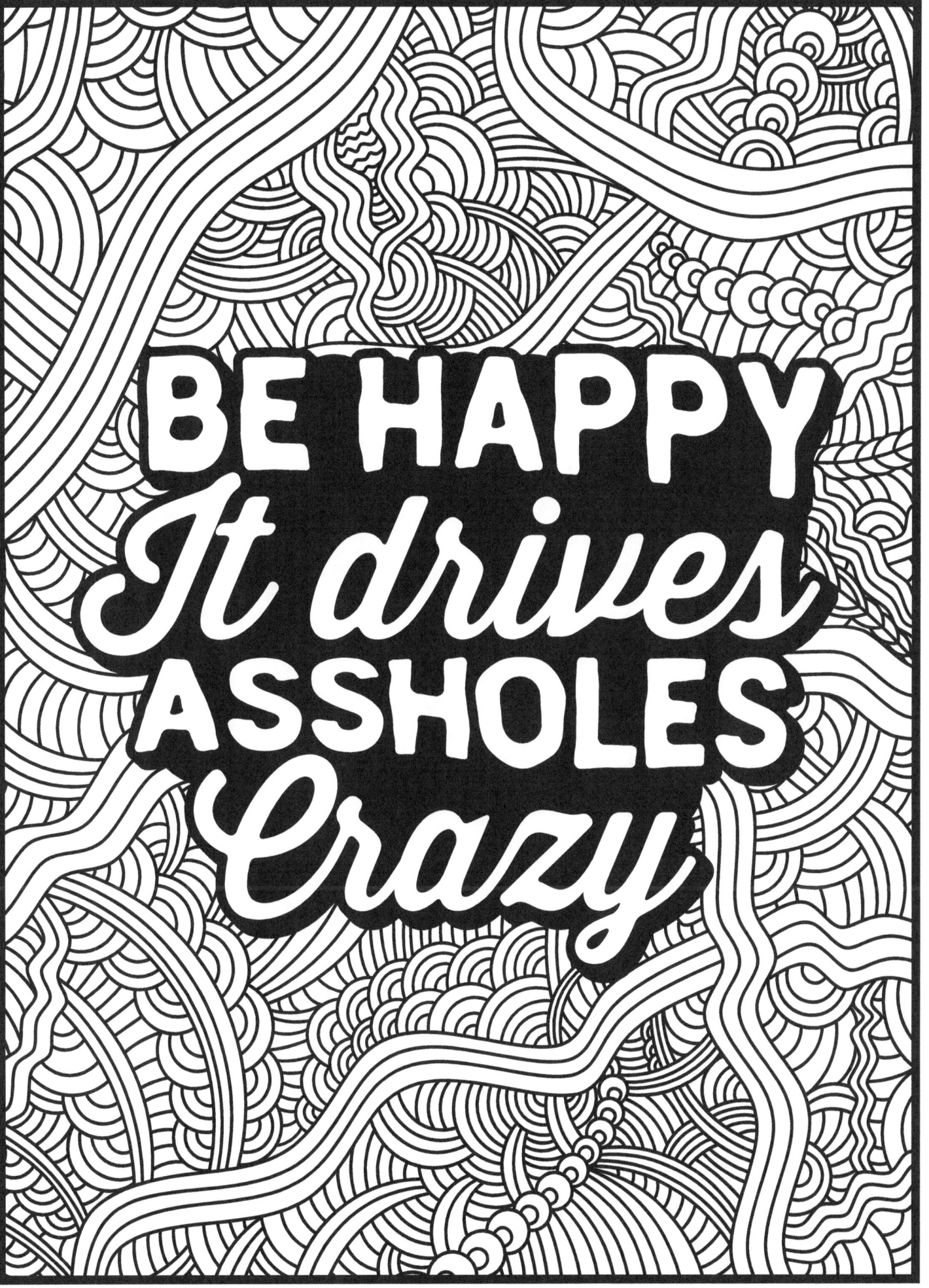

Colorful Swearing Dreams
Swear Word Coloring Book for Adults

Colorful Swearing Dreams
Swear Word Coloring Book for Adults

Colorful Swearing Dreams

Swear Word Coloring Book for Adults

Colorful Swearing Dreams
Swear Word Coloring Book for Adults

Colorful Swearing Dreams

Swear Word Coloring Book for Adults

Colorful Swearing Dreams

Swear Word Coloring Book for Adults

Colorful Swearing Dreams

Swear Word Coloring Book for Adults

Colorful Swearing Dreams

Swear Word Coloring Book for Adults

Colorful Swearing Dreams

Swear Word Coloring Book for Adults

Colorful Swearing Dreams

Swear Word Coloring Book for Adults

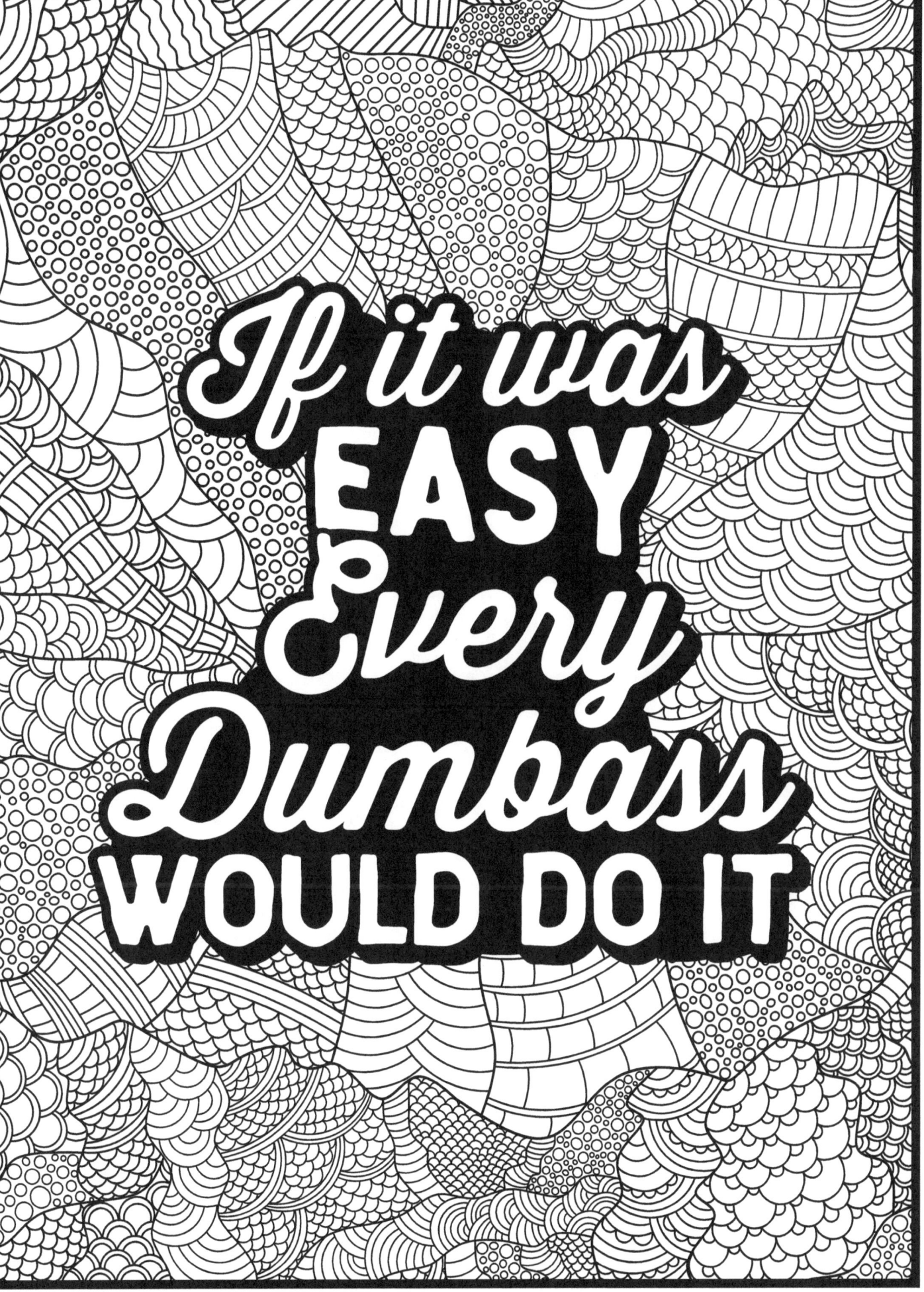

Colorful Swearing Dreams
Swear Word Coloring Book for Adults

Colorful Swearing Dreams
Swear Word Coloring Book for Adults

Colorful Swearing Dreams

Swear Word Coloring Book for Adults

DON'T HANG OUT WITH FUCKWITS

Colorful Swearing Dreams

Swear Word Coloring Book for Adults

DON'T WASTE your Energy on SHITS you can't CONTROL

Colorful Swearing Dreams

Swear Word Coloring Book for Adults

DOn't fucking quIT

Colorful Swearing Dreams

Swear Word Coloring Book for Adults

You're born a **GENIUS**, Don't let **DIPSHITS** ruin you

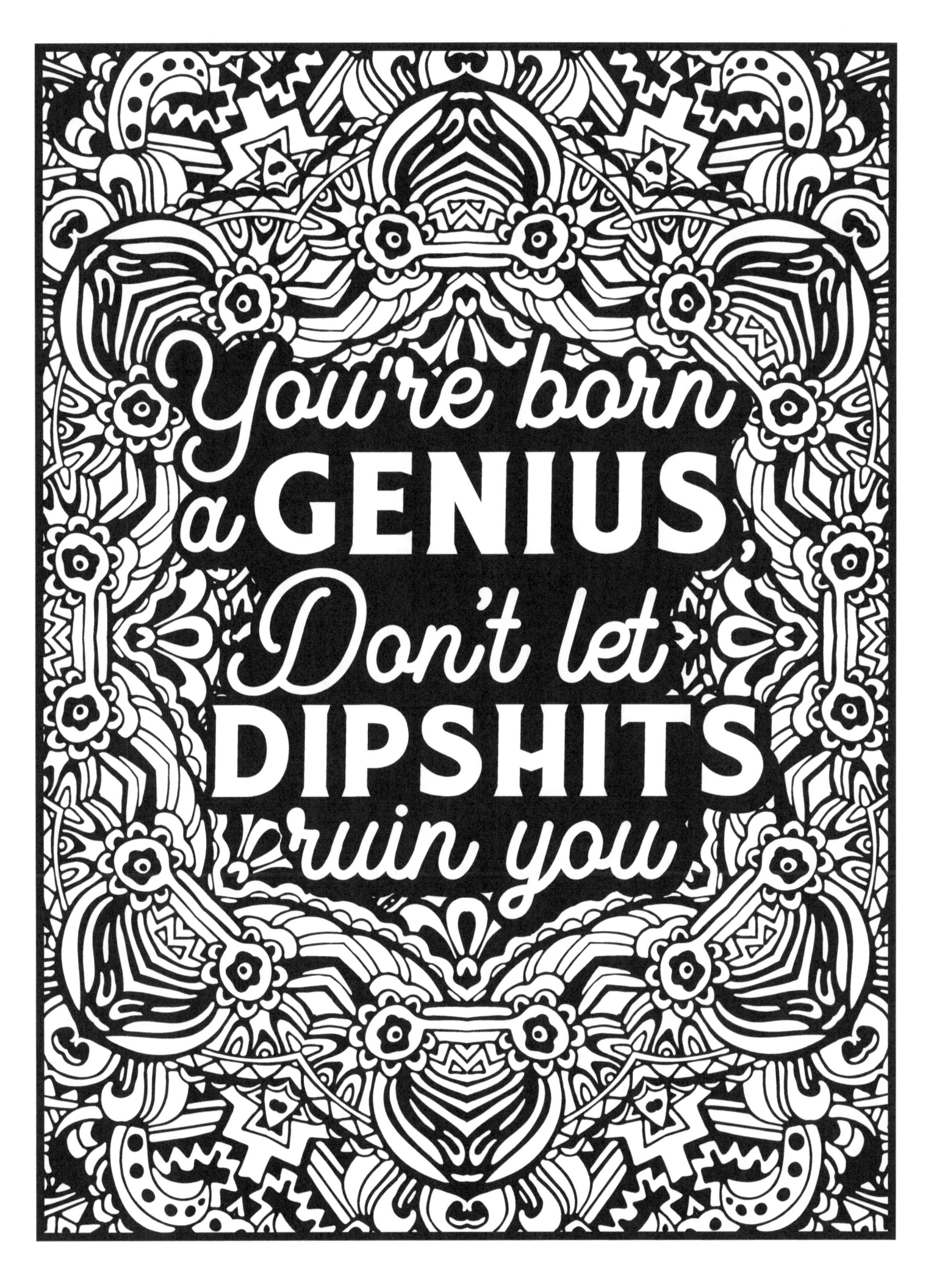

Colorful Swearing Dreams

Swear Word Coloring Book for Adults

STOP WASTING TIME ON BULLSHIT

Colorful Swearing Dreams

Swear Word Coloring Book for Adults

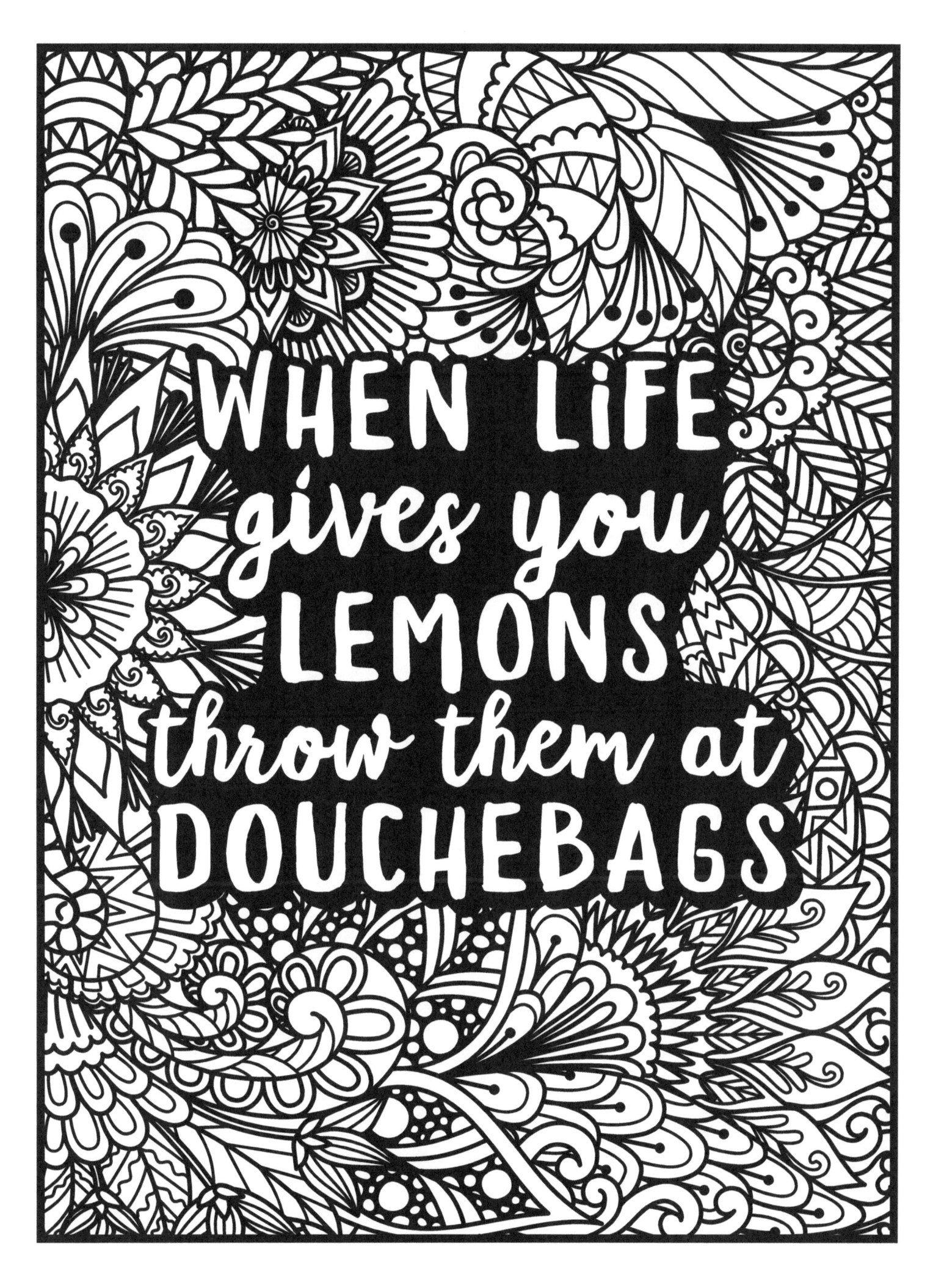

WHEN LIFE gives you LEMONS throw them at DOUCHEBAGS

Colorful Swearing Dreams
Swear Word Coloring Book for Adults

Of course Life is a **BITCH**, If it was a **SLUT**, it would be **EASY**

Colorful Swearing Dreams

Swear Word Coloring Book for Adults

SOME ASSHOLES ARE LIKE CLOUDS, WHEN THEY DISAPPEAR, IT'S A BEAUTIFUL DAY

Colorful Swearing Dreams

Swear Word Coloring Book for Adults

EXPECT THE BULLSHIT BUT NEVER ACCEPT IT

Colorful Swearing Dreams

Swear Word Coloring Book for Adults

Get rid of the NEGATIVE TWATS in your life

Colorful Swearing Dreams

Swear Word Coloring Book for Adults

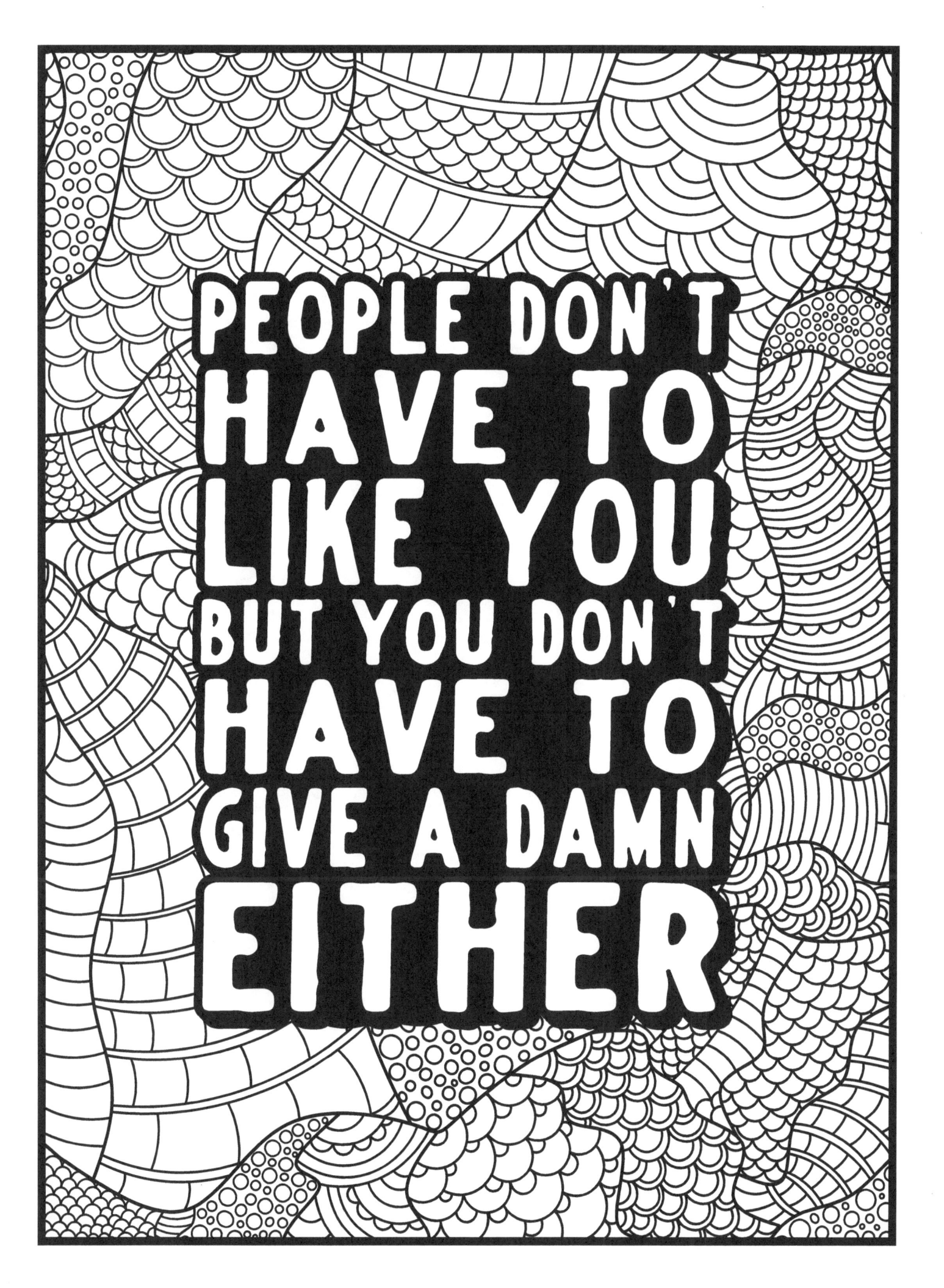

PEOPLE DON'T HAVE TO LIKE YOU BUT YOU DON'T HAVE TO GIVE A DAMN EITHER

Colorful Swearing Dreams

Swear Word Coloring Book for Adults

LIFE IS TOO SHORT TO FUCK IT UP

Colorful Swearing Dreams

Swear Word Coloring Book for Adults

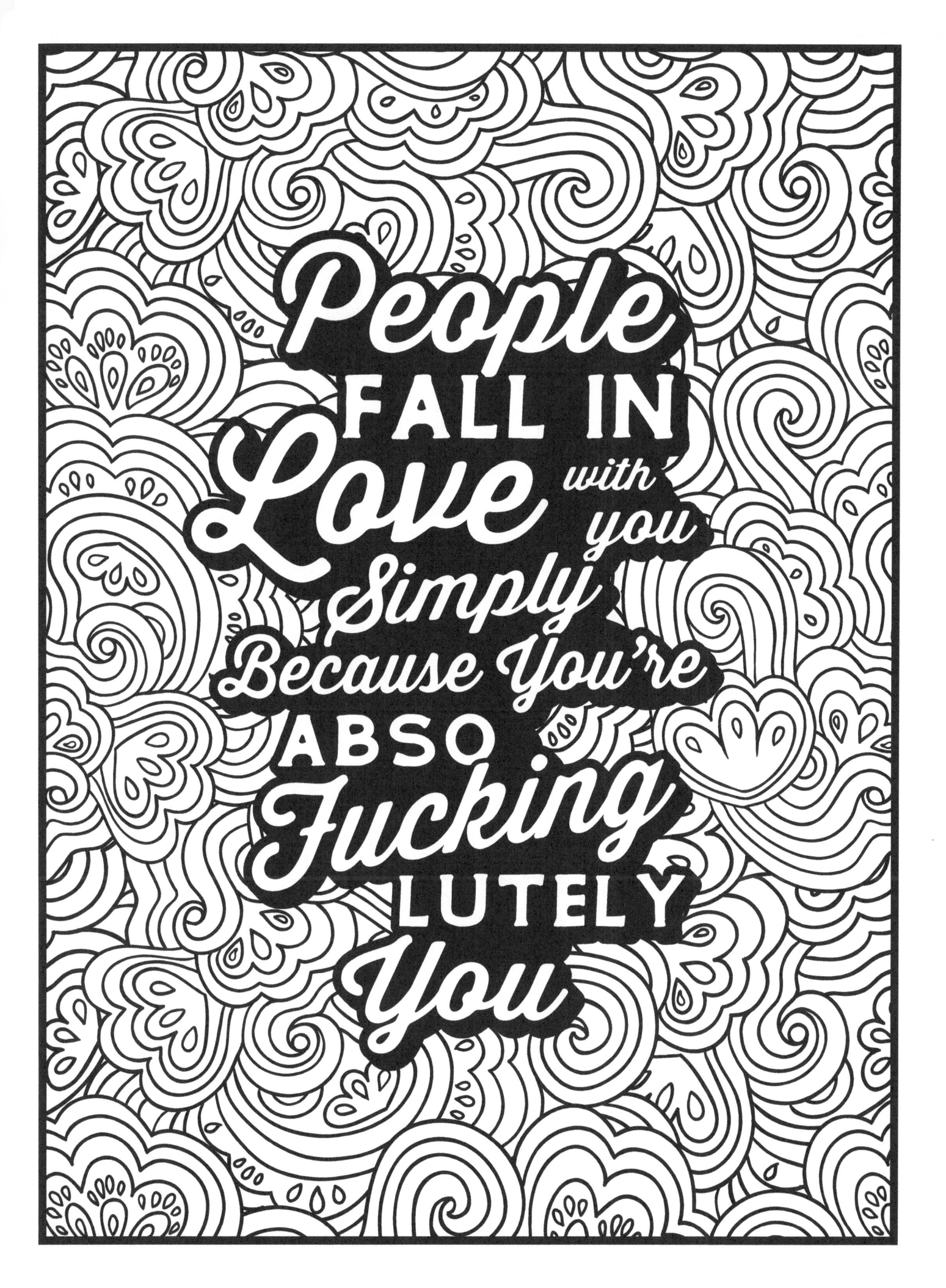

People fall in Love with you Simply Because You're Abso Fucking Lutely You

Colorful Swearing Dreams

Swear Word Coloring Book for Adults

NO ONE is entitled to treat you like SHIT

Colorful Swearing Dreams

Swear Word Coloring Book for Adults

Colorful Swearing Dreams

HOW IS YOUR STRESS LEVEL NOW?
WOULD YOU BE KIND ENOUGH TO REVIEW OUR BOOK?

Did the book allow you to put all the stress out of your mind, body and soul?
Hopefully you now feel fulfilled, relaxed and happy.

YOUR REVIEW is extremely valuable to us.

Your opinion, not only **helps other customers** to make the right decision but it also allows us to **make other quality products.** The type of gifts that make your friends and family laugh out loud !

We take pride in making quality products for your satisfaction.

That is why, we would really appreciate if you can take few minutes of your time and **leave us a review** on our product's page.

Create Review

Self-Love Positive Thoughts & Swear Words: Inspirational Quotes & Motivational Coloring Book ...

Overall rating
☆☆☆☆☆

JUST SCAN THE QR CODE WITH THE CAMERA APP ON YOUR PHONE

All Rights Reserved. Colorful Swearing Dreams

No part of this book may be reproduced, stored in a retrieval system, or transmitted in any form or by any means, electronic, mechanical, photocopying, recording, or otherwise, without the prior written permission of the author.

Colorful Swearing Dreams

If you liked this book, you'll definitely like our Best Sellers :

(just scan the QR Codes with your Camera app on your phone)

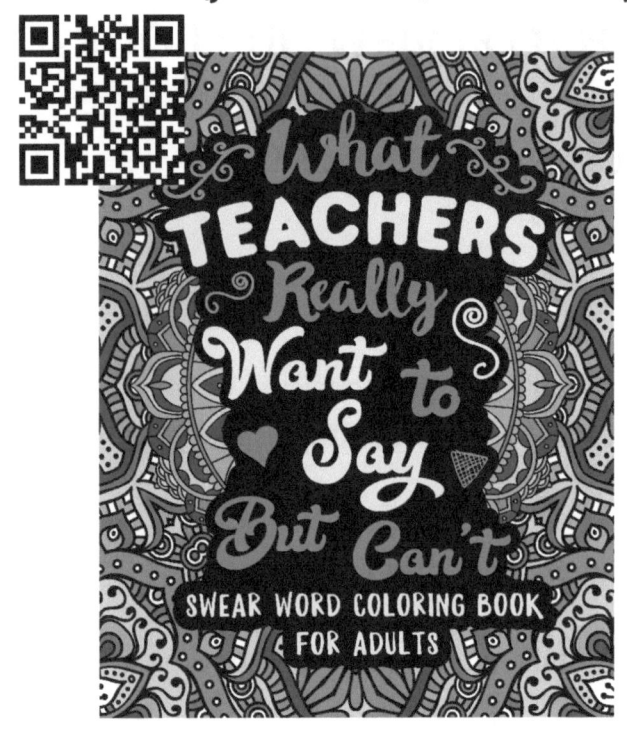

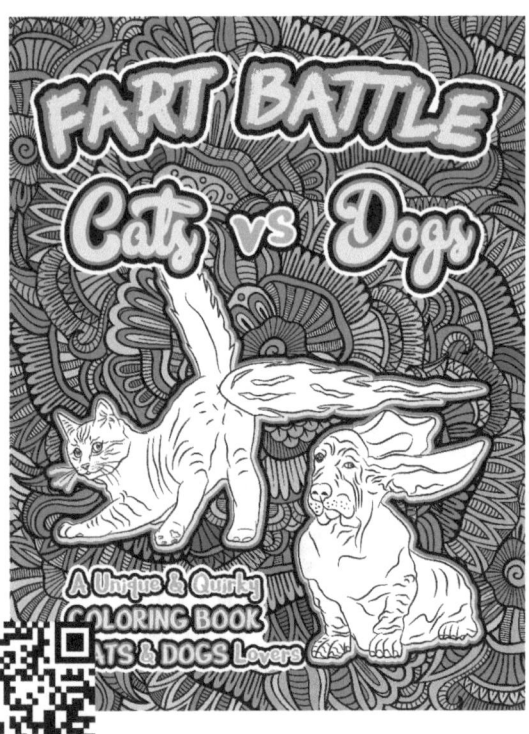

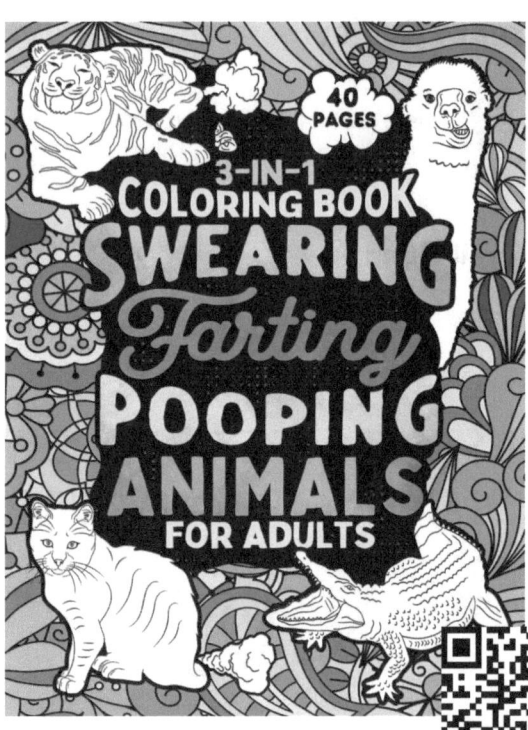

All Rights Reserved. Colorful Swearing Dreams

No part of this book may be reproduced, stored in a retrieval system, or transmitted in any form or by any means, electronic, mechanical, photocopying, recording, or otherwise, without the prior written permission of the author.

Made in United States
Troutdale, OR
11/09/2024